Summer

Monica Hughes

www.raintreepublishers.co.uk

Visit our website to find out more information about **Raintree** books.

To order:
- ☎ Phone 44 (0) 1865 888112
- 🖹 Send a fax to 44 (0) 1865 314091
- 💻 Visit the Raintree Bookshop at **www.raintreepublishers.co.uk** to browse our catalogue and order online.

First published in Great Britain by Raintree, Halley Court, Jordan Hill, Oxford OX2 8EJ, part of Harcourt Education.
Raintree is a registered trademark of Harcourt Education Ltd.

© Harcourt Education Ltd 2003
First published in paperback in 2004
The moral right of the proprietor has been asserted.

Editorial: Charlotte Guillain and Diyan Leake
Design: Michelle Lisseter
Picture Research: Maria Joannou and Liz Savery
Production: Lorraine Hicks

Originated by Dot Gradations
Printed and bound in China by
South China Printing Company

ISBN 1 844 21338 2 (hardback)
07 06 05 04
10 9 8 7 6 5 4 3 2

SBN 1 844 21343 9 (paperback)
08 07 06 05 04
10 9 8 7 6 5 4 3 2 1

British Library Cataloguing in Publication Data
Hughes, Monica
Summer
508.2
A full catalogue record for this book is available from the British Library.

Acknowledgements
The publishers would like to thank the following for permission to reproduce photographs: Alamy Images pp. 21, 23a; Bruce Coleman Collection p. 6; Bubbles pp. 8, 15, 20 (Grant Pritchard); Collections pp. 9 (Mike Kipling), 14 (Roy Westlake), 19, 23f (John D. Beldom); Corbis p. 7 (Ariel Skelley); Derek Laird/Still Moving Picture Co. p. 13; FLPA p. 23c (Ray Bird); Holt Studios pp. 5, 12, 17, 18, 23b; Oxford Scientific Films pp. 11, 23g; Sally & Richard Greenhill p. 23e; Trevor Burrows Photography p. 10; Trevor Clifford p. 4; Tudor Photography p. 22; Woodfall Wild Images pp. 16, 23d (Paul Hicks).

Cover photograph of a girl playing at the seaside, reproduced with permission of Impact (Bruce Stephens).

Every effort has been made to contact copyright holders of any material reproduced in this book. Any omissions will be rectified in subsequent printings if notice is given to the publishers.

Contents

Some words are shown in bold, **like this**. You can find them in the glossary on page 23.

When is summer?

It is never clear when one season ends and the next one begins.

Summer is the season after spring and before autumn.

We say that summer starts on 21 June.

June, July and August are the summer months.

What is the weather like in summer?

Summer is the hottest season of the year.

The sun is directly overhead and there are clear skies and high clouds.

If no rain falls there can
be **drought**.

We need to water the garden.

What clothes do we wear in summer?

We wear light, cool clothes in summer.

T-shirts, shorts and sundresses are good to wear in hot weather.

Sandals and flip-flops help keep our feet cool.

It's a good idea to wear a hat to protect yourself from the sun.

What happens in towns in summer?

People enjoy eating outside in the summer sunshine.

Many families leave the town to go on holiday.

Sometimes there are long **traffic jams** because so many cars are leaving the town.

What happens in the country in summer?

Crops ripen in the sunshine and farmers start to **harvest** them.

There are lots of country shows during the summer.

Farmers get a chance to show off their animals and meet their friends.

What foods do we eat in summer?

Strawberries are ready to pick and eat in the summer.

We can also eat fresh tomatoes and other vegetables.

We can enjoy salads and cold foods outside, especially ice cream!

What happens to insects in summer?

There are lots of insects to see in summer.

Bees are busy collecting **pollen**.

We can find butterflies and ladybirds in most gardens.

What happens to plants in summer?

Summer is a time when plants grow very well.

There are lots of brightly coloured flowers.

The trees are now covered
with leaves.

You can see every **shade** of green.

What celebrations are there in summer?

On 21 June, Midsummer's Day, there is a special celebration.

People go to a place called Stonehenge to watch the sunrise.

There is a **carnival** in London at the end of the summer.

There is a **procession** of dancers in wonderful costumes.

Make a butterfly print

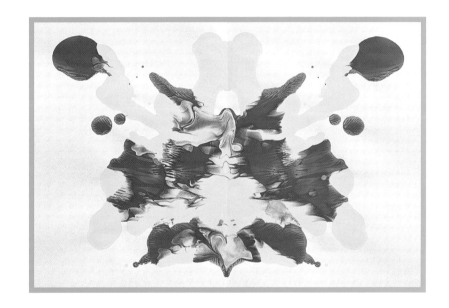

Fold a sheet of paper in half, open it out and drop paint onto one half.

Fold the paper over the paint and press down.

Open out the paper to see your butterfly.

Glossary

carnival
street procession with people singing and dancing

crops
plants grown for food

drought
when the land gets very dry because there is no rain

pollen
the yellow powder inside flowers

procession
lines of people moving along one behind the other

shade
different colour

traffic jam
when there are so many cars on the road they cannot move

Index